Magical Mythology

Magical Mythology

Fascinating Stories of Epic Characters

STUTI GUPTA

An imprint of
Srishti Publishers & Distributors

Srishti Publishers & Distributors
A unit of AJR Publishing LLP
212A, Peacock Lane
Shahpur Jat, New Delhi – 110 049
editorial@srishtipublishers.com

First published by
Srishti Publishers & Distributors in 2020

10 9 8 7 6 5 4 3 2 1

The stories in this book are based on the folk, performative, oral, written and various other versions of epics and other scriptures.

Dedicated to
my heart
and my soul...

My husband Vipul,
And my son Amay.

In loving memory of my brother Nikhil,

who went away too soon.

Till we meet again...

Contents

Contents

HANUMAN

KRISHNA

DRAUPADI

PANDAVAS

Acknowledgements

I have always believed in the power of gratitude. It can make people feel special, and motivate them to do good each day. I take this opportunity to thank all those who have made this book possible.

My son, Amay – He made me a storyteller by refusing to eat or sleep without a new story, every single day. Khushee and Yajas joined hands with him and made me dig out all these lovely tales.

My husband, Vipul – He is my backbone, my partner in crime and the one to make sure I keep rediscovering myself, without any compromises.

My big, happy family (touch wood) – The three sets of my parents – by birth, by love and by law, and the rest of the Guptas and Sharmas. Their selfless love is beyond doubt the best gift of god. A special shout-out to Akshima for helping me make this book more interesting.

Mr J.K. Bose, Arup, Vijay ji, Disha and the entire team at Srishti Publishers, my second home. They continue to give me all the love and support I need, even on the craziest days.

Prof T.S. Satyanath, who took me deep into mythological studies, especially the Ramayana. Sakshi Soni, for enlightening me with her findings and research on Draupadi.

Mr R.K. Mehra, who is a mentor par excellence, and pushed me into the vast sea of mythological studies, watching over me at all times. Kapish Mehra, for his words of encouragement and criticism – it helped me grow immensely.

Prof Kapil Kapoor, who held my hand and led me into the world of Indian mythology and poetics, of which he is a master.

Ishan Trivedi, for the delightful illustrations inside the book and on the cover. The figures could just wake up and talk!

Thank you Naveen ji, for making the book look so gorgeous and for bearing with me.

And most importantly, my little readers. You reach out to me and spread such joy, and also motivate me to write more. I hope you like this book as much as I have loved writing it for you.

Lots of love,
Stuti

Ganesha

Ganesha means the lord of all beings

His mount is a mouse

Son of Shiva and Parvati

Ganesh Chaturthi is celebrated in his honour every year

His consorts are Riddhi, Siddhi and Buddhi

His weapons are axe, noose and goad

His brother Kartikeya is also a god

He has two sons – Shubh and Laabh

1

A little adventure with Vishnu

It is believed that Ganesha was created by Parvati using turmeric paste rubbed from her body. She then breathed life into him and there he was - the son she always wanted! His first meeting with Shiva was not very amicable and the result was Shiva cutting Ganesha's head off with his *trishul* (trident). To make up for his mistake, Shiva put the head of an elephant on the child's torso and called him Ganesha. The child was also given the special blessing to be worshipped before all other gods and goddesses. The stories you will read now are a few of his exciting adventures in the world of gods and humans.

Ganesha was quite dear to uncle Vishnu, who often came to see him and also guided him in the godly ways. Known as a prankster, Vishnu was Ganesha's favourite uncle, and they had a lot of fun together.

Let's read how Vishnu had a little adventure with Ganesha.

Vishnu once came to Mount Kailash to meet Shiva, and discuss some important issues regarding the universe. When Vishnu reached, Shiva was playing with Ganesha. Both of them were laughing and having fun, just like any other father and child. Vishnu felt bad at disturbing them in their game, but it was an important matter. Little Ganesha was very happy to see uncle Vishnu. He met him fondly, and was happy that Vishnu had got *modaks* for him. Modaks were little laddus that Ganesha loved. You know, during the festival of Ganesha Chaturthi, modaks form an important part of the puja offering to Ganesha.

Shiva welcomed Vishnu and asked him to join them in their little game of hide and seek. Vishnu was surprised to hear about their game. Shiva was a powerful god, and his third eye enabled him to see what nobody else in the world could ever see. How could anyone hide anything from him? But Ganesha seemed to be winning here. So Vishnu politely said no to the game and requested Shiva for some time. Ganesha happily went to share his box of modaks with other *ganas* (followers of Shiva).

Sometime later, Vishnu sensed there was something wrong. He looked around and realized that his lethal weapon, the *chakra*, was nowhere to be seen. The same chakra had been used by him to destroy demons, and it could be dangerous if not handled properly. Knowing Ganesha to be a very naughty kid, he looked around to make sure he hadn't taken it. Just when his eyes found him, he saw Ganesha swallowing the chakra. Vishnu broke into a run, but before he could stop him, the chakra was gone; into Ganesha's stomach! Vishnu was shocked. If it had been someone else, Vishnu would have torn open their stomach to get the chakra back. But Ganesha? No!

He finally had an idea! He had heard from Shiva that Ganesha's laughter could shake the entire universe. Vishnu decided to try his luck and make Ganesha laugh. And then, guess what happened? Vishnu knelt down in front of Ganesha and started making funny faces. Ganesha was instantly diverted by Vishnu's antics and started copying him. Vishnu held his ears and made funny faces, poking his tongue out; he even made weird sounds to make Ganesha laugh. Finally, after a whole lot of effort, Ganesha started laughing out loud. So loud that the entire mountain shook. A little more effort and a little more loud laughter, and out came the chakra from Ganesha's mouth. Vishnu caught it immediately and went back to his home in Vaikunth.

Be it gods or humans, turns out laughter helps everyone.

2

Vishnu's wedding and Ganesha's plan

Ganesha was well-known for his immense love for food. He could eat anything, anytime. Once he was invited by Kuber for a meal, and he had eaten everything the king and the kingdom had to offer. Ever since, the gods were scared to invite him home. It was funny how Ganesha had emptied Kuber's palace and eaten the entire ration in a few minutes. The next story also tells us about Ganesha's love for food.

The gods were very happy. Vishnu had finally found the love of his life – Lakshmi – and a date had been decided for their wedding. Everyone in Vaikunth, where he lived with his followers and fellow gods, was very happy. Lakshmi is the goddess of wealth and prosperity, and Vishnu is the preserver of the world. Everyone thought it would be the perfect match.

Invitations were sent out, preparations were done, and the stage was set. The *baaraat*, or the marriage procession, was to reach Lakshmi's house and then bring her to Vaikunth after all the ceremonies. But there was one problem. A number of gods had come and requested Vishnu the same thing. While everyone respected Shiva and Parvati greatly, they did not wish to take Ganesha along with the baaraat. They knew that when it came to food, there was no stopping Ganesha. How insulted would they feel if one of the gods kept eating and eating? But Vishnu loved Ganesha, his nephew, very much. He paid no attention to these requests, until some of the gods refused to go with him if Ganesha was going. Vishnu was confused, and like always, came up with a trick to get out of the messy situation.

He went to Ganesha and told him that there was nobody in the whole universe who Vishnu could trust more than him.

And since Vaikunth was full of riches, food and expensive things for the new bride, he wanted Ganesha to keep a watch over Vaikunth while Vishnu and the party went to bring Lakshmi. Ganesha was delighted that his uncle Vishnu had trusted him so much and agreed immediately. He felt proud that he had been given an important task.

When the baaraat left, Narad muni came to Ganesha. Now, Narad muni is a learned sage, who is also a messenger between the three worlds – heaven, earth and the nether world (*svarg lok*, *mrityu lok* and *nark*, respectively). He came and told Ganesha the truth and also suggested a plan to make the gods and Vishnu realize their mistake. Ganesha was very sad to know the truth, and agreed with Narad muni to teach everyone a lesson.

The plan involved several mice, all friends of Ganesha's mount. An army of mice dug up the path that Vishnu and the baaraat were to take, and covered it up with some leaves. The road looked clear and the singing and dancing baaraat did not notice anything wrong. But the moment Vishnu's chariot crossed that patch, the wheel went down into the pit and got stuck. Many efforts by the entire army of gods couldn't bring it out.

A peasant was passing by, and witnessing the scene, he offered to help. The gods were sure that this human wouldn't be able to do anything when the gods were failing, and ignored him. But when he was given a chance, the peasant chanted Ganesha's name – *Om shri Ganeshay namah* – and

lifted the wheel. It came out in one go! The moment of realization had come. The gods realized their mistake and prayed to lord Ganesha for forgiveness. Ganesha was happy again, and blessed everyone. That is how the baaraat could proceed and Vishnu could marry Lakshmi.

Once all of them came back home, Ganesha welcomed his aunt Lakshmi lovingly, and Vishnu beamed, the proud uncle.

Family is the most precious gift one can get. We must always stand by our loved ones - in good, and not-so-good times.

3

The magical fruit

We have often seen Ganesha on a mouse, but have you wondered why he has such a simple mount, while other gods have powerful or very beautiful ones. Once a demon named Gajasura obtained a boon from Shiva, that he could be killed only by someone as dark as him. Since he could change himself into anything, it was impossible to defeat him. The gods were fed up of the crazy things this demon did, so lord Shiva sent Ganesha to take care of him. When Gajasura realized he would be defeated, he changed himself to a mouse so that he could run away. But Ganesha defeated him and spared his life, deciding to have Gajasura as his mount in the form of the mouse, so that he never forgot his lesson.

The following story tells us how this mount has taken little Ganesha on the best of journeys.

One morning, Narad muni came to Mount Kailash with a divine fruit. He was happy to see Ganesha and his brother Kartikeya also there. Kartikeya is a strong god, who is also the General of the army of gods. He is worshipped for his strength and limitless energy.

Narad muni was very happy to see both the children, but also went quiet all of a sudden. Shiva and Parvati knew that it could only be some confusion that had silenced Narad muni. Otherwise he talked so much that one had to ask him to stop. When asked, Narad muni told Shiva and Parvati that he had got a divine fruit. He had not known Kartikeya would be there and hence had only one. And there was a little problem – the fruit couldn't be cut or divided in any way, otherwise it would lose its magic. So the only way was to give it to one of the kids.

This put Shiva and Parvati in a dilemma too. They did not want to favour any one child and leave the other. So they decided to have a small competition. Whoever won would get the fruit – fair and square! It was decided – the task was for the children to take three rounds of the world, and whoever came back to the parents first would get the fruit as a prize.

Kartikeya is a war god, and his mount is the peacock. He was sure he would be the first to complete the race, so he sat on his peacock and flew away without wasting any time. Little Ganesha was left standing near the mouse, wondering how he could win. The mouse looked at him, as if requesting Ganesha to not make him run so much. Three rounds of the world for a race – without food or water. "Oh no", the mouse thought.

After giving the matter some thought, Ganesha came up with a plan. He sat on his mouse and went around his parents thrice. Shiva, Parvati and Narad were confused and asked him what he was up to. Ganesha lovingly said that his parents were his world and he wouldn't go and find it anywhere else.

Stumped by Ganesha's wisdom and smartness, Narad muni patted his back for his thoughtfulness and declared him the winner. While Ganesha won the magical fruit and ate it, Kartikeya was a little angry when he came back. But he was also impressed with Ganesha. He loved him so much that the anger ended then and there.

Anger eats into our positive energy. We should try to take the negatives into our stride and focus on the happy things.

Mounts and friends of the gods

Let's find the names of some animals that our gods love.

M	A	C	R	O	W	F	G	J	U	S	V	N	C	B
E	O	D	U	T	O	R	T	O	I	S	E	D	B	G
R	Q	U	D	I	P	J	E	K	G	T	Q	T	U	S
T	D	R	S	G	L	G	S	W	A	N	F	V	F	A
A	F	V	T	E	C	T	P	V	R	A	M	A	F	G
P	B	B	A	R	R	D	L	B	U	L	L	H	A	N
I	Y	U	A	W	O	H	G	D	D	L	I	V	L	B
G	N	P	E	A	C	O	C	K	A	K	T	O	O	S
E	U	A	N	T	O	R	E	G	R	P	K	U	N	P
O	L	R	J	H	D	S	Q	A	S	X	V	D	R	Y
N	K	R	U	Y	I	E	A	E	N	F	S	R	E	E
Q	I	O	C	E	L	E	P	H	A	N	T	H	F	V
S	P	T	S	V	E	Y	V	P	K	W	B	K	J	H
C	D	E	R	Z	A	U	Y	V	E	Y	Y	V	J	E
T	A	N	T	E	L	O	P	E	Y	C	A	M	E	L

*There are 20 names hidden in this grid.

Rama

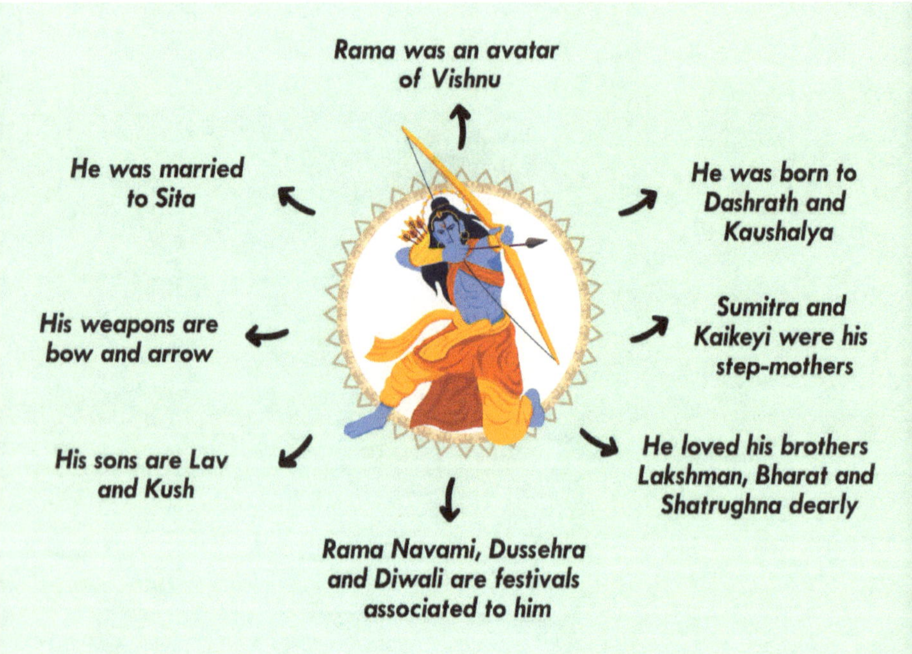
Rama was an avatar of Vishnu
He was born to Dashrath and Kaushalya
Sumitra and Kaikeyi were his step-mothers
He loved his brothers Lakshman, Bharat and Shatrughna dearly
Rama Navami, Dussehra and Diwali are festivals associated to him
His sons are Lav and Kush
His weapons are bow and arrow
He was married to Sita

4

When Rama wanted the moon

The *Ramayana* is one of the most popular epics in India. Believed to have been written by Maharshi Valmiki in 1st century B.C., it is presented in the form of a poem in 24,000 verses. The childhood of Rama and his brothers – Lakshman, Bharat and Shatrughna – is discussed in the Uttara Kanda.

King Dashrath had three wives – Kaushalya, Sumitra and Kaikeyi. But all three queens had no children. So the sages in the court of Ayodhya suggested that the king and his queens perform a Vedic sacrifice – a *Putrakameshti yajna* – to pray for children.

Following that yajna, the king and queens were blessed with four sons. The boys played together, ate together, and made the palace and the kingdom of Ayodhya a happier place. The following is one such story from Rama's childhood that is very popular in folk literature. It will surely bring a smile to your face.

Rama and his brothers were playing together in a chamber in the palace, specially designed for the little boys. There were monkeys made of soft silken cloth, and horses made of wood. They would ride these horses and pretend that they were going to battle like their father, the mighty King Dashrath. After all, they were growing up listening to stories of his wisdom and bravery.

When Sumitra and Kaikeyi called out to the children for their dinner, Rama wondered why he hadn't heard mother Kaushalya's voice calling out to him. Just as his brothers ran out for their meal, Rama sat down on his favourite chair near the window, staring at the stillness outside.

The window opened into a garden, with the most beautiful flowers and trees, but he could see nothing as it was dark. Just then, he heard the honey-sweet voice of his dear mother. Rama's face lit up with happiness when he saw mother Kaushalya entering the room with a bowl of his favourite food in her hands – *kheer!* Plus, dinner time was Rama's favourite, because his mother told him many stories while he ate. Stories of brave kings and gods, of magical creatures and dangerous demons – he dearly loved them all. He waited eagerly for his mother to tell him a story while she fed him.

Kaushalya came and stood next to Rama's chair, gently patting him on his head, asking him if he was ready for the story. Rama nodded excitedly and Kaushalya sat down opposite him, giving him spoon after spoon of kheer. She loved how little Rama's eyes opened wide as the story progressed. She was narrating the story of the moon tonight. How the moon had been cursed by lord Ganesha once. She noticed that Rama was staring at the moon, without blinking.

She tried to distract him, but it was of no use. Rama continued staring at the full moon, glowing in the white light. He looked so divine that Kaushalya went ahead and kissed little Rama's forehead. The touch finally brought him back from his thoughts and he turned towards his mother with a strange request. He wanted a new toy, and mother Kaushalya lovingly promised to get it for him the very next morning. But he wanted it now. He wanted the moon! Kaushalya laughed, but seeing the serious expression on Rama's face, understood that he really wanted the moon.

She knew he had a strong resolve, just like his father, and would not give up till he got what he had asked for. She had to think of something, and quickly. Rama's eyes were now wide open and slightly teary. Kaushalya took him into her arms, hugged him tight and asked him to wait a bit.

A few minutes later, in walked two attendants. One with a small stool in her hands, and the other with a huge pan. Rama guessed the pan was full, because the attendant was walking slowly and carefully. The first one put the stool on

the floor near Kaushalya, and the second one swiftly put the huge pan on it. Rama peeked in and saw water in it.

Kaushalya sat little Rama down and asked him to look into the water. He could see his own reflection. He jumped up and ran to stand behind his mother. With the change in position, and a clearer view of the water, Rama finally saw what Kaushalya was trying to show him – the beautiful reflection of the full moon. Little Rama was very happy and hugged his mother for the lovely gift.

Wasn't it very intelligent of his mother to fulfil his wish like this? And did you know, in another version of the same story, Kaikeyi is believed to have shown Rama the moon in a hand-held mirror.

It is wonderful to see little kids curious about nature around them, and it is even more lovable when parents figure out new ways each day to bring a smile to their children's faces.

A parent can do anything for their child. It is most essential to understand their love and respect them.

5

Rama, Sita and their swimming competition

When he grew older, Rama had won Sita's hand in marriage. Rama had broken Shiva's mighty bow – called Pinaka – to impress Sita and her family. You will read this in detail in the pages to come. After the marriage, the newly-wed couple was living happily in Ayodhya. That's when Rama's stepmother Kaikeyi asked for two boons from King Dashrath. He was known to keep his promises and assured Kaikeyi that her wish would be granted, whatever it may be. So when Kaikeyi asked for her son Bharat to be crowned the king of Ayodhya after Dashrath, he had to agree. Even though he always wanted to see his eldest son Rama as king, he was bound by his promise.

Her other wish stated that Rama would have to spend fourteen years in exile (*vanvas*), away from the kingdom.

Rama could not bear to see his father break his promise. So, as a dutiful son, Rama accepted this and prepared to leave Ayodhya. Sita decided to go with him. Lakshman insisted on being taken along. The following story is from their time in the forest.

After Rama left the palace for the forest with Sita and Lakshman, the people of Ayodhya tried to stop them from going too deep into the forest. They thought that if Rama would agree to stay in the woods just on the outskirts of their kingdom, they would be able to take better care of their beloved princes and princess. But Rama did not think it was a good idea. He felt if he stayed too close to the people of Ayodhya, then they would never accept Bharat as their king.

So they left the kingdom and travelled far in search of a suitable place. When they reached the Dandakaranya forest, they instantly knew it was going to be their new place to live. Birds chirped the whole day, trees sang with the breeze and it was a pleasant feeling to be there. A lake nearby ensured that they had plenty of water for all their needs.

Rama and Lakshman set out to collect some wood, branches and dried grass to make a hut. Sita, on the other hand, started searching for twigs, dried wood and other things that would help her make a fire for cooking. She also unpacked some fruits that they had collected on their way.

Once they settled in, they went out to explore their surroundings. Knowing what the forest around them was like would help protect themselves from any wild animals.

When they reached the lake, they were all mesmerized by the beauty of it. The dark clouds in the sky were reflected in the lake's clear waters. While Rama and Lakshman were standing on the bank, Sita had walked ahead and stepped into the water. The two brothers watched as Sita ventured deeper into the water. Soon enough, she seemed to be floating. She turned around and smiled seeing the shocked expression on their faces. She laughed out loud and challenged Rama to a swimming competition.

Rama and Sita had both been trained to swim as a part of their education, so Rama readily agreed and followed her into the lake. He handed over his bow and arrow to

Lakshman. They decided that Lakshman would be the referee for the race.

As Lakshman signalled them to start, both Rama and Sita started off, each ahead of the other. Lakshman had to keep his eyes focused, without blinking, so as not to miss who would actually win in the end. Both of them were amazing swimmers and guessing who would win was impossible. Just then, Rama noticed that Sita was having some trouble swimming because of her clothes. One layer of her saree was draped around her arm, which was making it difficult for her to swim properly. Rama slowed down a bit to help her untangle the piece of cloth restricting her arm. Sita saw Rama getting momentarily distracted and swam harder. As a result, she reached the other end of the lake first.

Lakshman was happy to announce Sita as the winner, and Rama was taken aback. But then, they all laughed and proceeded towards their new house to start a fresh life.

Life will put us in tough situations often. The key is to never give up and keep trying.

6

Goddess Durga blesses Rama

Did you know, the *Ramayana* has many versions. It is fascinating to know that a lot of these adaptations were done keeping in mind the people who would hear these stories. Like we tell children only those stories that we know they are fond of.

For instance, in the south Indian versions, Ravana is a very brave king. He rules his kingdom well and keeps his people happy. Also because south India is closer to the so-called 'Lanka' geographically, there is more charm associated with the 'hero' from the neighbourhood.

Similarly, in north India, which is closer to the birth place of Rama, there is more hero worship of Rama and his brothers. In the same way, we see a leading presence of goddess Durga in the Ramayanas from east India. We will read in the chapter to come how in a Bengali *Ramayana*, Sita took the form of goddess Kali to kill the thousand-headed Ravana.

In the story that follows, we see Rama performing a yajna, a prayer ceremony, to appease goddess Durga.

The sun was about to set and the ocean water in front of Rama was painted red. The waves touched his feet, but he was lost in deep thought. From winning Sita's hand in a swayamvar, to welcoming her to the royal palace; from the exile in the cruel forest to her being kidnapped by the rakshasa king Ravana – he felt the last few years had been too unfair to Sita.

Lakshman came and stood near Rama lovingly. He wanted to ask his elder brother why he looked so sad. After all, they had found Sita and were going to set her free soon. Rama told him how much he missed his wife and how worried he was for her. He was really hoping that they would be able to meet her soon and take her back to Ayodhya.

Ram also told Lakshman how they were now ready for battle. Nala and Neel – the two architects from the *vanara* army – had completed the task of building the bridge to cross the ocean. The vanaras and other leaders in the army were fully prepared too. Now Rama wished to offer his prayers to gods, to make sure he had their blessings to win the battle against the powerful Ravana, his brother and sons.

When the sun rose the next morning, Rama prepared to hold a yajna near the seashore. He set up flowers, fruits, milk, pure water and other essentials he could gather in the forest

to worship goddess Durga. He lit the fire in the *yajna kund* and started chanting mantras to invoke the goddess. He was to chant the mantras 108 times, and offer one lotus flower at the end of each set to successfully complete the ritual.

He sat there alone, performing the puja. It was soon early evening and he was reaching the end of his puja. He had offered 107 lotus flowers when he realized there were no more flowers left to be offered. The ritual would not be complete without 108 offerings, and he was short of one.

One of Rama's names is 'Kamala-nayan', which means 'having lotus-like eyes'. Since he had always heard people praising him for his lotus-like eyes, he decided to complete the yajna by offering his eye as the 108th lotus.

He stood up and held the sharp arrow in one hand, ready to pluck out his eye. Sensing his resolve and the purity of his feelings, and happy with his sincere puja, goddess Durga appeared in front of him. She blessed Rama to be victorious in battle. Rama was happy and bowed down to thank the goddess. Now he was sure – no matter what happened, he would win this battle and rescue his beloved wife Sita.

❖

In one version of the *Ramayana,* after Rama completes this yajna and is ready for battle, he looks worried. On Lakshman's asking what the concern is, Rama explains that they need to seek blessings from a brahmin for the yajna to

be complete. They were in a battlefield – all warriors, vanaras and several others. Where would they find a brahmin here? That's when Rama and Lakshman saw a man in a brahmin's clothes walking towards them. Everyone around them suddenly started whispering. Vibhishan came closer to tell the brothers that this was Ravana himself.

Lakshman wanted to charge at him, but Rama stopped him. They enquired why Ravana was there and that too as a brahmin? Ravana explained that he was the only brahmin for miles around and he had come to bless Rama, so that his yajna could be complete.

Rama bowed down to seek his blessings, and Ravana blessed him – "*Viajayi bhava!* Let victory be yours." Everyone around them was surprised to hear those words. He blessed Rama and returned to Lanka to get ready for battle.

Don't you think it was strange and also good of Ravana to do that?

Black and white, good and evil are all two sides of the same coin. To be good, you only need to defeat the not-so-good inside you. As simple as that!

Hanuman looks very happy sitting on his tail.
Let's colour the picture and have some fun.

Sita

Sita was born out of the earth

Sita Navami, Dussehra and Diwali are festivals associated to her

She was brought up by Janak and Sunayani

Her sons are Lav and Kush

She had three sisters – Urmila, Mandavi and Shrutakirti

She was married to Rama

7

The birth of Sita

Worshipped as an ideal wife, a warrior princess, and a doting mother, Sita is best known as a goddess of prosperity and abundance. While some see her as an epitome of sacrifice and someone who gave up all riches and comforts for her duties as a wife and daughter, some others also see her as the reason behind the battle of the *Ramayana*.

There are some versions of the epic that state that it was prophesied even before her birth that she would be the cause of Ravana's death – the king and ruler of the rakshasa race. In some other retellings of the epic story, we see how it was Ravana's own karma, unlawful activities and pride that took him to his end. To begin with, let's start with knowing some interesting stories behind Sita's birth.

According to the *Valmiki Ramayana*, king Janak was a powerful leader who ruled over Mithila. His kingdom was peaceful and the people were happy with the king's governance. His people loved and respected him immensely, and he ensured their comfort in every way. His only worry was that he did not have a child. When some sages in his court suggested that he conduct a Vedic *yajna* (a spiritual sacrifice/ *puja*) for begetting a child, he and his wife Sunayani readily agreed.

A piece of land was chosen for the *yajna* and Janak decided to plough it on his own as an offering. A huge number of people from the kingdom gathered to witness their dear king performing the ritual, and to wish him luck. Just as he had begun to plough the land, his plough hit something hard and did not move any further, even with great effort from Janak and his wife. No matter how hard they tried, they just could not move the plough.

In a bid to not leave the yajna in between, Janak sat down and started clearing the soil around the plough, which was stuck in the earth. That is when he found a golden casket buried there. He was surprised. When he actually dug it out and opened it, he was shocked to see a beautiful baby girl in it. He was sure the baby had been sent to him by the

gods. He picked her up in his arms and beamed with joy. He decided to name her Sita. (*Seet* is a Sanskrit word which means a furrow – a small trench made by the movement of the plough.) Sita was adoringly brought up, along with her three sisters in Mithila, under the watchful eyes of Janak and Sunayani.

The earth is often considered as a metaphor for fertility and abundance, and that is why many readers of the *Ramayana* have interpreted Sita's presence in the narrative as an epitome of fertility, abundance and joy.

In certain later, regional variations of the *Ramayana*, Sita is seen as an incarnation of Vedavati. Ravana had set her eyes on Vedavati and tried to make her his wife, while she was performing penance as a *tapasvini.* In order to save her chastity, she had jumped into the *havan*, holy fire. She had chosen to end her life, as against marrying Ravana, who had tried to force himself upon her. She had cursed Ravana before dying that she would be born again and be the end of him. And thus, she was born as Sita.

In some narratives, Sita is also shown to be Ravana and Mandodari's daughter. The sages in his court had warned Ravana and prophesied that their first born daughter would be his end, so he had asked a trusted minister in his court to go and leave the child somewhere far away. He had, in turn, put the child in a casket and placed it on the land which was to be ploughed during the yajna. That is where Janak found her.

Not just that, it is worth noting that Sita – the daughter of the earth – also went back to her mother earth in the end of *Valmiki Ramayana.* In the section called Uttara Kanda, which is the last section in the epic, when Rama again questions her chastity, she is heartbroken. She prays to go back to where she had come from. And the earth splits open and swallows Sita forever. In her birth and end, Sita is truly the daughter of the earth.

We all need to stay grounded in life. No matter how high we reach, we must never forget our roots.

8

Princess Sita and Pinaka

It is common knowledge that royal children were given a thorough knowledge of Vedas and other scriptures, along with rigorous training in use of weapons and warfare. Similarly, Sita and her three sisters – Urmila, Mandavi and Shrutakirti – were also well trained in scriptures and warfare.

Sita was also seen as a warrior princess worthy of a most deserving prince. Let's read and find out how king Janak faced a rather tough situation when Sita was just a child.

There is a small episode in *Valmiki Ramayana* which is of great interest and importance today. God Devendra created two bows of infinite energy and might, named Sharanga and Pinaka. They were equally powerful in all respects and it was tough to decide which one would outdo the other in battle. These two bows were made for the two most popularly worshipped gods in the Hindu pantheon – Vishnu and Shiva, respectively. Brahma suggested a duel between the two to judge which bow was more powerful, but just when they were about to begin, there was a divine announcement (*akashvani*), that their battle could destroy the creation of gods – the earth, people, animals and everything else.

Considering it to be a valid concern and to avoid any such dangers in the future too, Shiva threw Pinaka from the heavens above to the earth below. The fall had a powerful impact, but the bow remained intact.

It was eventually discovered by king Devaratha, an ancestor of king Janak of Mithila, that is Sita's father. Since then, Pinaka had been kept in the royal palace, in a special chamber, and nobody was permitted to go there. It anyway required a number of people to move the bow around, so nobody could have thought of stealing it or misusing it.

One day, Janak was walking down the corridor, towards the court, when he heard his daughters chuckling and talking in a garden. They were talking, playing and giggling loudly while running after one another. He noticed Urmila, Mandavi and Shrutakirti, but Sita was nowhere to be seen. He looked around for her and noticed her walking into the chamber where Pinaka was kept. Curious, he also went towards the same place, and tried peeping in from behind the curtain. What he saw next shocked him completely. Sita was examining Pinaka curiously, while holding it up in her hands, as if it was a toy. His surprise knew no bound, especially because he remembered he himself had been able to pick up the Shiva *dhanush* only with great effort. And here was Sita – holding it like it belonged to her.

The episode made Janak quite anxious about his beloved daughter and her hidden capabilities. He was advised by some sages and senior ministers in his court that the same bow be kept as the condition for her *swayamvara* when the time came.

So, ultimately, when the swayamvara actually happened, Rama – the prince of Ayodhya, the son of Dashrath – was the only one who could pick up the Shiva dhanush named Pinaka. He even ended up breaking it while trying to string it. That is how he most deservingly won the warrior princess's hand in marriage.

9

When Sita killed Maya Ravana

The *Ramayana* has popularly come to be seen as a battle between good and evil. But as you know, there are many versions of the *Ramayana*. There were many renderings written on the regional level – like *Kittibasi Ramayana* from Bengal and *Kamba Ramayana* from Karnataka, among others. It is fascinating to read how the same epic story changes drastically when adapted by a particular region.

The *Adbhuta Ramayana* is one of the most interesting renderings of the story. *Adbhut* in Sanskrit means wonderful or fascinating. And as the very name suggests, the epic is also remarkable. The following episode from the same shows us a ferocious face of Sita, and the extent to which she could go to save her husband's life.

Sita was standing in front of Rama in the court at Ayodhya, surrounded by all chieftains and ministers. She had been abducted by Ravana while she was in exile with Rama and Lakshman. Rama had travelled all the way to Lanka, crossed the ocean, and defeated Ravana to free Sita from his clutches. Now back in Ayodhya, Rama had taken over as king and there were celebrations all over. But, Sita disclosed something that changed everyone's happiness to anxiety.

Sita told everyone that while she was still in Mithila with Janak, a *brahmin* passing through their kingdom had told the king about Ravana's older brother – Sahasra Ravana. As per the sage, he had a thousand heads and was more powerful than Ravana. On hearing this, Rama, Lakshman, and Hanuman decided to wage war against him and proceeded towards an island called Pushkar, where he was supposed to live.

Once there, Sahasra Ravana fought with all his might, and after a tough battle, had wounded both Rama and Lakshman. When Sita saw Rama fainting in the battlefield, she was very angry. But everyone present saw her laughing loudly and uncontrollably. All the soldiers stopped dead in their tracks to see why she was laughing like that. They

could not believe their eyes when they saw Sita taking the form of Maha Kali. With a third eye, and breathing fire, she looked like death itself. In a blink of an eye, Sita as the horrific goddess Kali had slashed all the thousand heads of Sahasra Ravana and killed him. She had ended the battle in a moment.

But such was her anger at Rama's losing consciousness, that she continued killing whoever came in her path. Even the gods were scared to see her. At this rate, she would destroy everything. The gods then requested Shiva to intervene and stop her. Shiva came to their rescue, and revived both Rama and Lakshman.

Rama was very scared to see Sita as Kali and could not understand if it was really his sweet wife. Shiva came and lay down under Kali's raised foot and absorbed the great blow, along with all her anger. That brought her back to her original form as Sita.

Having defeated the thousand-headed Sahasra Ravana in this way, Sita returned to Ayodhya with Rama and the rest of the army.

When you see an otherwise polite person being rude and aggressive, don't jump to conclusions. They might be struggling, and looking for someone to support them.

Can you guess the right names?

1. Lord Ganesha's favourite food

	O			K

2. The Preserver in Hindu mythology

	I		H		U

3. Shiva's mighty bow is called

P			A		A

4. Shiva's beloved mount, the white bull

	A			I

5. Vishnu's mount, a bird

	A		U		A

6. A small bowl that could produce unlimited food

A					Y

	A		R	

7. The river in which Kaaliya naag lived

	A			N	

8. The teacher of Kuru princes and Pandavas

D			N	

9. The snake-king's daughter

	L			I

10. Name of lord Rama, which means "having lotus-like eyes"

	A			L

N		Y		

Ravana

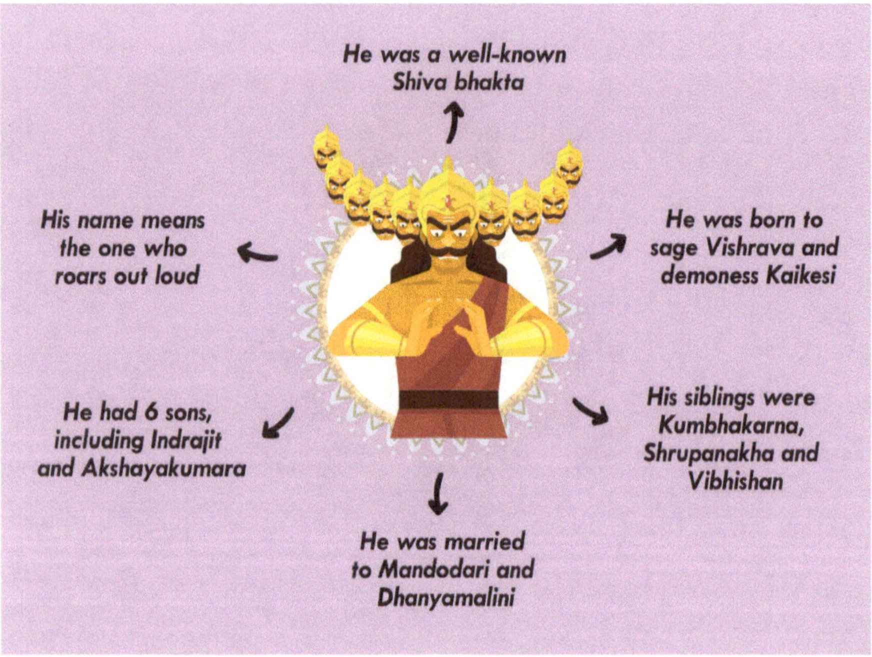
He was a well-known Shiva bhakta
His name means the one who roars out loud
He was born to sage Vishrava and demoness Kaikesi
He had 6 sons, including Indrajit and Akshayakumara
His siblings were Kumbhakarna, Shrupanakha and Vibhishan
He was married to Mandodari and Dhanyamalini

10

Ravana and Shiva – the showdown

Ravana in the *Ramayana* was a mighty ruler and a fierce warrior. He was the king of the rakshasas. We all know he abducted Sita and lost his family and kingdom in the battle with Rama. But there are several other things that Ravana did, that not many know about. For instance, did you know Ravana is the most celebrated Shiva bhakta ever? Or that he was the one because of whom the Mahabaleshwar Temple *shivlinga* was established? The stories you read here are some such unheard aspects of Ravana.

Ravana's brother Kuber was the king of Lanka before Ravana conquered it and made it his home. After losing Lanka, Kuber set up his home in Alaka city. But the new city was so charming and attractive that Ravana went ahead and won that over too.

He was excited at being the king of another beautiful city and was returning to Lanka on his Pushpak Viman – the flying vehicle that flew on his mind's command.

While flying back to Lanka, he noticed a beautiful mountain looming ahead. It had such pretty flowers and trees laden with fruit, that he was tempted to stop and see more. He was wonderstruck – what place was it, and how could there be so much flora and fauna on such a cold, snow-laden mountain! But then suddenly, his plane stopped abruptly. Now Pushpak was a magical plane, so when it stopped and didn't start moving despite Ravana's trying hard, he was confused. It hadn't ever happened before. Pushpak had never disobeyed him. Ravana saw a bull on the mountain and got down to talk to him.

The white bull was Shiva's beloved mount, Nandi. Ravana told him about his plane and asked him if he could help fix it. Nandi explained to Ravana that this was Mount Kailash and nobody could fly over it, as it was Shiva and Parvati's home. Basically it was a no-fly zone as it was a powerful god's residence.

Ravana was not used to hearing a no from anyone. His ministers and family knew that once he set his heart on something, he would do everything to have it. He had just won over a beautiful city after defeating his brother, now he thought he would do the same to Mount Kailash. Little did he know that things were going to change for him, quite a bit.

You must not forget that Ravana was indeed very powerful. He had performed *tapasya* (penance) for years and had earned a lot of special super powers. The only flaw in him – which led to his downfall later – was his pride and the unjust use of his power. Full of confidence, he hopped onto the Pushpak Viman, and went to the base of the mountain. Nandi tried to warn him kindly, requesting him to not disturb the gods. But when Ravana did not stop, Nandi tried to stop him by force. Ravana defeated Nandi using his magical powers and still went ahead.

Once at the base of the mountain, Ravana took on a huge form – with ten heads and twenty arms, more powerful than thousands of elephants put together. Bubbling with energy and proud about his magical powers, he picked up the entire Mount Kailash like it was a feather. He roared out aloud, like a warrior who had just defeated his enemy.

The mountain shook, and with it shook Shiva and Parvati. In fact, goddess Paravati lost her balance and was about to

fall, but lord Shiva saved her just in time. Seeing her worried face, he assured her that she should not worry and that it was the doing of one of his bhaktas. Parvati couldn't believe a bhakta would do such a thing. But looking at Shiva's mysterious smile that she doted over, she wasn't worried anymore. She knew he would take care of everything.

Still smiling, Shiva pressed Mount Kailash down with his big toe. Yes, just the big toe. And that was enough. It made Ravana roar again – this time, in pain. The mountain had come down on him so suddenly that now he was stuck beneath it. He was pinned under Mount Kailash, with Shiva sitting on it, smiling his mysterious smile.

Ravana was in immense pain, and did not see any way to get out of this problem. What do you think he will do?

Nandi saw Ravana in pain and told him to leave his pride aside and sing praises of Shiva. Only then he would be able to free himself.

Did Ravana listen to Nandi this time? Did he sing Shiva's praises? Turn the page to find out!

There is a thin like between confidence and over-confidence. We must not cross the line if we wish to grow in life.

11

Ravana becomes a Shiva bhakta

Not seeing any other way out, Ravana concentrated all his powers on Shiva, who had done this to him. What he saw enlightened him and changed him. Here he was, in pain and struggling; and then there was lord Shiva, sitting calmly, smiling, and pressing the mountain down with his big toe. Ravana realized that no matter how strong or powerful he was, Shiva would always be a step ahead. After all, Shiva is known as the all-powerful Destroyer in the Hindu mythology (teaming with Brahma, the Creator and Vishnu, the Preserver). Let us now read how Ravana came to be known as the most celebrated Shiva bhakta ever.

Although stuck under Mount Kailash, Ravana thought of ways to free himself. Nandi told him to bow down to Shiva, and surrender himself to god. Since Ravana had been missing for long now, some of his ministers came looking for him. When they saw Ravana in such a helpless state, they couldn't believe their eyes. They heard Nandi's idea, and agreed that it was the only way out.

In extreme pain and realizing his folly, Ravana is believed to have sung praises of Shiva for many many years. He knew he had met someone far ahead of him in power, and he put his faith in Shiva completely. When finally lord Shiva was happy with Ravana's bhakti, he released Ravana and let him go back to Lanka.

In these years, Ravana is believed to have sung the entire *Shiv Tandav Stotra* – 1008 extempore hymns worshipping lord Shiva. Interestingly, he is also believed to have used one of his ten heads along with one of his twenty arms to create a musical instrument. His tendons worked as the strings of the instrument and he used it to give music to his hymn. Shiva was so impressed with the sincerity with which Ravana was singing that he released him and accepted him as his bhakta.

Till date, a bowed string instrument is used in accompaniment to folk music in India, Sri Lanka and surrounding areas. It is called Ravanhattha (Ravana + *hatha*/ hand).

Since then, Ravana has come to be known as one of the most dedicated devotees of Shiva. He is also believed to have sacrificed all his heads to Shiva in trying to gain boons from him. It goes to show his resolve and patience to pursue what he really wanted. In an otherwise villainous representation of Ravana all through the *Ramanaya*, this one characteristic is positive and awe-inspiring.

No matter how many flaws someone has, they will also always have some qualities too. It is for us to encourage the growth of the right qualities.

12

Sita was Ravana's daughter

We have just read how Janak found Sita and adopted her as his daughter. She was raised like a princess and given all that she desired.

But what would you say if I told you that Sita was Ravana's daughter? Some versions of the *Ramayana* actually tell us that. But then, why would he kidnap his own daughter? Let's find out!

Ravana was eagerly looking forward to the birth of his child. When the baby girl was born, Ravana was very happy. The glow on the baby's divine face brightened up his face too. But the astrologers and priests in his court predicted that this child would bring Ravana's end. She would lead to his clan being wiped out. He was in a dilemma. No matter how much he loved the child, he could not ignore the prediction and put his people's lives at risk.

So upon the court priest's insistence, Ravana ordered the child to be taken to a far-off land. A few messengers carried her away and buried her in the earth. That is where king Janak was performing a yajna, and dug her out. You have already read about this in the last few pages.

When Ravana found out years later that his daughter had survived, he was overjoyed. He loved her dearly and had sent spies to find out about her. She was a princess married to a handsome and brave prince. What could be better?

Everything was well till Rama was exiled and sent to live in a forest. Ravana could not bear the fact that his daughter was living in a forest. She deserved a royal life. After all, she was the daughter of the king of rakshasas. To make sure she had all the comforts, Ravana abducted her and brought her to Lanka. But Sita was heartbroken. She wanted no comforts; she wanted only Rama.

When Rama challenged Ravana in the battlefield, Ravana started losing his sons and ministers while fighting with the vanara army. Mandodari asked Ravana why he was being so stubborn. She knew if Ravana went into battle, he would be killed.

Ravana lovingly told Mandodari that he wanted to give his daughter Sita to Rama, and wanted to make sure she lived happily with him. But after losing all his family in the battle, if he did not go out to fight, it would be very selfish of him. He wanted to take the battle to its end and be defeated at the hands of Rama.

Dying at the hands of the avatar of Vishnu would give him the *moksha* he had been praying for.

We all know how the battle ended; we all know Ravana as 'evil'; we all know Sita went back to Ayodhya with Rama. In these episodes, I have tried to share some unknown events about Ravana, which show the other side of him.

All good is hard, all evil is easy. We have to choose wisely in all our life situations.

Hanuman

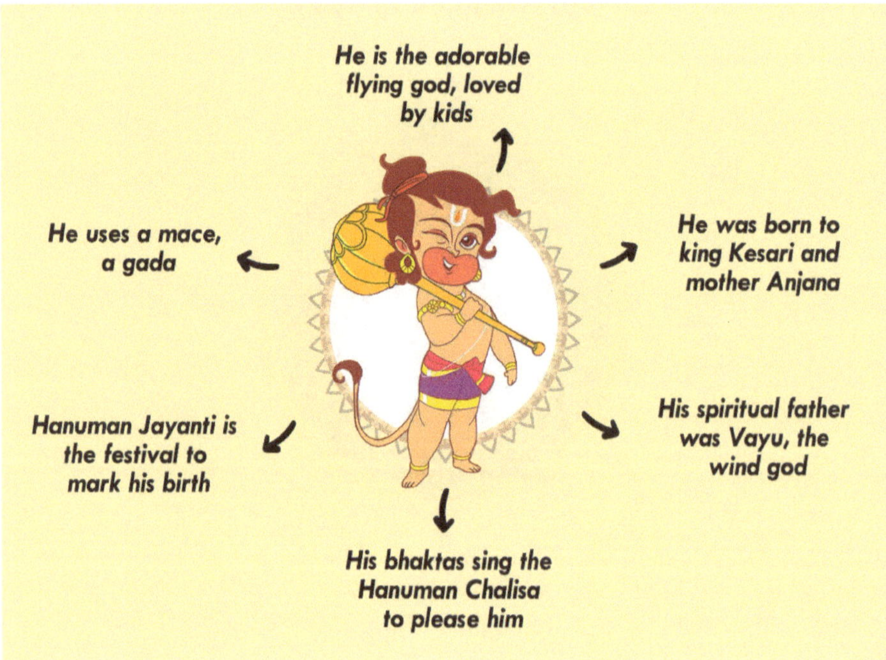
He is the adorable flying god, loved by kids
He uses a mace, a gada
He was born to king Kesari and mother Anjana
Hanuman Jayanti is the festival to mark his birth
His spiritual father was Vayu, the wind god
His bhaktas sing the Hanuman Chalisa to please him

13

Hanuman in Ravana's court

Don't we all know how tough it would have been for Rama to find Sita's location, if not for Hanuman? Crossing the wide ocean in between and reaching Lanka on the other side, Hanuman entered Lanka without being noticed and found Sita in Ashok Vatika. He presented Rama's ring to her and assured her that she would be rescued soon. After making sure that she was safe, he offered to carry her back to the shore, to Rama, but Sita wanted to wait for Rama. So Hanuman took his leave, and decided to explore Lanka.

Hanuman now knew the details of how Sita had been kidnapped by Ravana and how she had been treated in Lanka so far. He would pass on all the information to Rama and the rest of the army. Now he wanted to go around Lanka, check their military camps and meet Ravana. He had a message to convey. So he went around Lanka, breaking towers, setting parts of the palace on fire and destroying many gardens.

Ravana was very proud of Lanka and its beauty, so when his soldiers told him that a monkey was destroying his city, he was very angry. He wanted to punish him and ordered his *sipahis* to go and capture him.

Several minutes later, the soldiers came in, breathless. They had been unable to catch the monkey. They said he could fly and change his form. Some said he was a *mayavi* – a magical creature with super powers. Ravana himself was very powerful and he knew he could capture the monkey in the blink of an eye, but if he went out, the people of Lanka would feel the monkey was really powerful. So he sent his son Indrajit to catch him. It took Indrajit great strength and a magical rope to capture Hanuman.

The one thing that nobody knew was that Hanuman had let himself be caught. He had been making such a mess to come face to face with Ravana. Indrajit proudly walked into the court, with Hanuman following him. Hanuman was set free and made to stand in the centre. He looked around and noticed that while some people looked shocked, some were amused to see a monkey in the court.

Ravana addressed him, asking him who he was and why he had been ruining his beautiful city. Hanuman could not help but notice the aura on Ravana's face. He decided to calmly explain why he was there.

The moment Hanuman declared that he was Rama's messenger and had just met Sita, all hell broke loose. Ravana turned red with rage. The court ministers started screaming for the monkey to be killed, so Hanuman told them all that he was a messenger, and as per battle principles, he could not be harmed. Ravana laughed out loud on hearing that. When Hanuman asked to be offered a seat, everyone else in the court started laughing too.

Indrajit mocked Hanuman and told Hanuman to sit on his tail, if he was so keen on sitting. While the others laughed, Hanuman took it seriously. He started elongating his tail. It kept growing and nobody could do anything about it. Soon enough, it had grown so long that Hanuman started coiling it to make a tower. Finally, when the tower had grown taller than Ravana's chair, Hanuman hopped up and sat on it.

It took everyone by surprise that the notorious monkey had done something like this. Hanuman looked at Ravana with a teasing expression and told Ravana and the court

members that he had let Indrajit capture him. He wanted to tell them that they should respectfully free Sita, or Rama and his army would defeat them and rescue her. It would mean destruction for Lanka and its entire people.

It was a shrewd reminder for Ravana that no matter how powerful he was, he could still be challenged.

Have you noticed in most Rama idols and pictures, how Hanuman is mostly sitting at Rama's feet? Sitting on a seat higher than Ravana's, in his own court, was a clear message that Rama and his army were fully capable of beating Ravana and his ego.

14

Hanuman with five faces: Panchamukhi Hanuman

Pancha (five) + *mukha* (face)

Out of the many forms in which Hanuman is worshipped, the Panchmukhi form is rare and fascinating. He is seen having five different faces and the secret behind it is being shared in the following story. It is important to understand here that Hanuman plays an essential part in the battle between Rama and Ravana. If not for Hanuman, Rama and Lakshman would have fallen prey to Ravana's tricks.

The battle between the armies under Rama and Ravana had taken a dangerous turn. Many soldiers from both sides were losing their lives each day. The battle had to come to an end now, so that each one could save their families and armies from further damage. Wars and battles never bring anything good, and the loss is immense in comparison to what is left in the end.

At this point in the battle, Ravana planned to play one of his tricks to kill Rama and Lakshman. He knew that if the leader was out of the way, the army would automatically surrender. Additionally, the news of Rama's death would also make Sita surrender to Ravana. He had a plan and he was sure it was going to work out in his favour perfectly.

Ravana had a brother named Ahiravan, who was the king of the nether world – *paataal lok*. Ravana planned to take Ahiravan's help to get the brothers kidnapped and killed. Once they entered the nether world, the brothers would never be able to come back to the earth on their own.

But there was a problem. Hanuman had made a fortress around the brothers, which nobody was allowed to enter. How would Ahiravan reach the brothers, leave alone kidnap them? Ahiravan was a mayavi too – he could change his form at will. So he took the form of Vibhishan, who was

Ravana's brother. Vibhishan was now Rama's most trusted partner. When Hanuman saw Vibhishan approaching, he let him enter without a question. It was only a little while later when Hanuman saw Vibhishan at a distance that he realized he had been fooled.

By that time, it was too late and Ahiravan had taken Rama and Lakshman to paataal lok. There was panic in the army, and nobody knew how to get the princes back. On the other hand, celebrations had started in Lanka, because Ravana had got news that Ahiravan had been successful.

On getting to know all the details, Vibhishan told everyone that it must have been Ahiravan. He also told Hanuman that someone would have to go to paataal lok and kill Ahiravan to save the princes. He said that Ahiravan could be killed in just one way and Hanuman would have to find a way to do that. Hanuman heard Vibhishan patiently and decided to go and rescue Rama and Lakshman.

Hanuman shrunk himself into the smallest size and slipped into paataal lok. As per Vibhishan's words, he started looking for the five lamps that held the life of Ahiravan. In order to kill Ahiravan, he had to blow out all the five lamps, at the same time. Since all the five lamps were kept in different directions, it was a tricky thing to accomplish.

Hanuman then took the form of five-faced Hanuman, also popularly known as *Panchmukhi* Hanuman to accomplish the task.

When he prayed to Brahma, Vishnu and Shiva to give him the means to defeat Ahiravan, along with his own head, four more heads grew out. Since Rama is believed to be an avatar of Vishnu, the following came to the rescue to save the lord.

1. Hayagriva – an avatar of Vishnu, he has a horse's head and a man's body.
2. Narasimha – Vishnu's avatar with a lion's head over a man's body.
3. Garuda – Vishnu's mount, a bird.
4. Varaha – a boar form of Vishnu that had rescued the earth.

Aided by these five heads, Hanuman was able to blow out the lamps in all five directions, at the same time. That killed Ahiravan, and Hanuman could fly back to the battle ground with Rama and Lakshman.

Don't let fear decide your future. If you are determined, you will find a way. Just like Hanuman did.

15

When Hanuman met Bhima

It has always amazed me to know that for hundreds and thousands of years, people have been doing tapasya (penance) to gain immortality – which means they would live forever, and never die. But the gods are also smart. They don't give the boon of immortality to anyone. After all, anyone with such a precious gift could be dangerous to the world.

Out of the many immortals who are known to us, who we read will live for as long as the world exists, one prominent name is Hanuman. It is believed he is present wherever the name of Rama is chanted. So moving on from the *Ramayana*, where he plays such a major role, we also see him featuring in the *Mahabharata*. Let's know more about it.

The Pandavas and Draupadi had now approached the end of their exile years. The dice game had landed them in the forest for a long time. Now they were sure of a battle with their own kin, and Arjun had gone to the Himalayas to perform tapasya. He knew very well that facing his gurus, powerful warriors and others from the Kuru army would not be so simple. He would need more divine weapons. In his absence, the rest of them decided to move to another forest, for a change of scene.

They reached a forest called Narayanvana, which welcomed them with flowers and fragrances. Draupadi was excited to be in such a beautiful place and they built their hut there. One day, the breeze wafted the intoxicating fragrance of a flower to Draupadi. Her heart was set on the flower and she asked Bhima to find out more about it and get one for her.

Bhima was more than happy to fulfil this small wish and headed out into the forest. On his way, he met a few wood cutters and asked them about the fragrance. They told him it was a flower called *saugandhika,* and also gave him directions to the pond where the flowers grew.

He had barely walked a few more minutes, following the fragrance, when he saw an old monkey sitting in the middle of his path. He tried to find a way around the monkey's tail, which was blocking the path, but the forest was so dense, he couldn't find anything except this narrow passage. So he asked the monkey to give him way. The old monkey did not move at all, and kept smiling to himself.

This annoyed Bhima, and he was very angry. He roared, 'Do you know who I am? I am Bhima, son of Kunti and the wind god, one of the Pandavas, and brother of Hanuman. I can crush you in a minute. Clear out my way.'

Hearing him roar, the monkey looked more amused than impressed. He sat up slightly and asked Bhima, 'Oh! Who is this Hanuman? What has he done that I should know him?'

Bhima was shocked at this monkey's ignorance. So Bhima told him that Hanuman was the one who had crossed the ocean and found Sita in Lanka. He and the *vanara sena* (monkey army) had helped Rama defeat Ravana and rescue Sita.

The old monkey kept smiling and told Bhima, 'Okay! You look like a powerful, well-built guy. I am just an old monkey. Why don't you pick up the tail and put it aside to make way for yourself?'

Bhima thought that would be better too. Why waste time arguing with a monkey! Bhima was a celebrated warrior, well-known for his strength and physical power. He thought this would be rather simple, but he was in for a surprise.

He bent down and tried to pick up the tail, but he could not even move it. He thought the monkey was playing a

prank, so he tried harder. He used all his might and strength, but still could not lift the tail. After trying for several minutes, he understood that this was no ordinary monkey. He bowed down and offered his apologies for being disrespectful and ignorant. He also shed his pride and surrendered at the monkey's feet to ask who he really was.

The monkey then stood up and hugged Bhima. The moment the monkey hugged him, Bhima felt a renewed energy in his body; like he had been given a powerful boost. The monkey then told him that he was Bhima's brother – Hanuman. He had come to see him to tell him that no matter how powerful Bhima was, he would have to leave his ego and pride in order to fight the tough battle that waited for them.

He also promised to be with Bhima all through the battle, and settle on Arjun's chariot flag to see them win.

When in a competition we believe the opponent to be better than us, we only work harder for victory.

Let's get little Rama the moon.
Want to add some colour to this?

Krishna

The blue god was an avatar of Vishnu

Born to Vasudev and Devaki, he was brought up by Nanda and Yashoda

Holi and Govardhan Puja are other festivals associated to him

Janmashtami is celebrated as his birth day

His siblings were Balaram, Subhadra and Yogmaya

His weapons include the Sudarshan chakra and Kaumodaki

His consorts are Radha, Rukmini, Satyabhama and several others

His children were Pradyumna, Samba and others

16

The universe in Krishna's mouth

If there is one god in Hindu beliefs who is so adorable, so popular, so notorious, so tricky and so different – it is Krishna. In his child form (Bal Gopal) and the grown-up phase, he stands out for his unique acts and naughty activities. Stories from Krishna's childhood can make up for an entire book in itself. He is cute, smart and very naughty. We all know he stole butter and ate it, hid people's clothes while they were bathing, and killed demons even as a child. Let us read another endearing story from his childhood days.

When Krishna was born and placed in Gokul with Nanda and Yashoda, the family did not know what an adventure their life would be… for years. Little Krishna used to get visitors – not just people of Gokul who came to see him and doted over him, but also dangerous demons like Putana and Kakasura, sent by Kansa. So out of fear for his life, Yashoda made it a point to keep Krishna with her, wherever she went. He would never go out of her sight.

On one such day, Yashoda was headed to the river for a bath and some washing. I am sure you know that back in those days, people had huge houses – with gardens and animal sheds, with big kitchens and open areas. But they did not have bathrooms, as we know them today. So they had to go to the river bank to bathe and wash their clothes. Can you think of staying in a house that doesn't have a bathroom? Or just telling your mother, 'Mumma, I need to take a bath. Let's go to the river bank.'

But anyway, little Krishna did not complain. He loved going to the riverside. Not just because he could enjoy an outing and play in the water, but also because he met his friends there. He would really look forward to it every day.

One morning, Yashoda settled him on the river side and told him to sit there and play. She wanted to fill a pitcher with water and give it to Krishna. They also did not have buckets, so a *ghada* was a perfect vessel for the purpose. Just as Yashoda went to the river, little Krishna sat in the mud, looking around, waiting for his friends.

Krishna heard a sweet voice calling out to him. He looked around but found no one. When he heard the voice again, he realized it was coming from the ground on which he was sitting. It was Mother Earth, *Bhu devi.* She was ecstatic that Krishna had set foot on her and wanted to seek his blessings. Not every day would she get a chance to meet an avatar of Vishnu, that too as an adorable little baby.

Krishna smiled and made Bhu devi even happier. But she felt bad that she had nothing to offer to Krishna. Mud and little stones was all there was, which she could not offer to the child. The thought made her very sad.

To cheer her up, little Krishna took a handful of mud and put it in his mouth, telling Bhu devi that he enjoyed whatever she had to offer. She was delighted and couldn't thank Krishna enough for having accepted her offering so lovingly. She took her leave and went away happy.

But Yashoda was not happy when she came back to Krishna. She could see his mouth full of mud and she panicked. Filling her hands with water from the pitcher, she cleaned his mouth from the outside, all the while scolding

him for having done such a thing. Krishna, on the other hand, kept smiling at the little adventure.

Then Krishna thought it was the right time to show Yashoda that her son was not an ordinary being, and she should not be scared of these little things. He opened his mouth when Yashoda asked to look in for more mud. And she was taken aback.

Inside the little child's mouth, she could see the whole universe – the sun, the planets, the unending atmosphere and all the big and small heavenly bodies. She started crying out of fear, thinking some other monster had possessed her baby. But soon, seeing how Krishna was smiling, she understood that her child was no ordinary baby. He was special. From that day on, she became more confident than ever that little Krishna could fight any evil that came his way.

Every mother thinks her child is a super hero in disguise. And heroes are made by the path they choose.

17

Krishna and Kaliya naag

In Gokul, Krishna was famous as a naughty child. He and his friends had a *toli* (a small gang), which used to be together all the time. They would play together, eat together, collect fruits together, go to open fields to graze their cows together – they were inseparable. The people of Gokul loved them all immensely, but Krishna was their absolute favourite. One day when Krishna vanished while playing, all hell broke loose. Let us find out what happened next.

Krishna and his friends were playing football on the river side. It was their favourite sport, and they used to have a lot of fun. Since Krishna always kicked the ball really hard and it went too far, the toli made a rule – whoever kicked the ball out of the decided boundary would have to go and get it too. It was a fair rule.

The ball with which they played was not any ordinary ball. Those days, balls were not available in shops for sale. People used old clothes, and tied them all together, layer on layer, to make a thick, hard ball. That was the kind of ball that Krishna and his friends were playing with.

Krishna kicked the ball and it went straight into the Yamuna river. That was surely out of the boundary, but the other kids could not even ask him to get it because it would have sunk into the water by now. They all looked really sad and angry with Krishna.

Little Krishna offered to go and fetch the ball. His friends thought he was joking and started laughing. But when they saw Krishna walking towards the river, they got really scared. They knew their friend Krishna very well – if he had decided, he would definitely go and get the ball.

Krishna walked towards the river. While some friends tried to stop him, several others ran to look for elders who

could stop Krishna. Unfortunately, by the time the elders came, Krishna had already jumped into the river.

Their ball was nowhere to be found, but Krishna saw a huge black snake. He remembered Radha also telling him about a snake that had scared her. Its name was Kaliya naag. Krishna asked the snake to give the ball back, and also told him to not scare people living on the banks of Yamuna ever again.

Kaliya naag refused to listen to Krishna, and to teach him a lesson, started binding him in the coils of his tail. The hold of the snake's tail was so strong that Krishna was unable to free himself. His breath was also running out with the pressure. Then, Krishna started expanding his size, to become bigger and bigger. Soon, he had become so big that Kaliya naag could not hold him anymore.

Just as Kaliya naag let him go, Krishna jumped on to the snake's head and took on the weight of the whole universe. The snake could not understand how the little child could be so heavy. So he continued to fight. And Krishna continued to beat him with his feet, the fangs of the snake crushed under his weight.

Kaliya naag gave up and surrendered, asking for forgiveness from the little boy. He brought Krishna up to the surface of the water, to put him down on the shore.

When Yashoda, Nanda and other people of Gokul saw Krishna dancing on the snake, they were scared and fascinated. Yashoda kept crying, out of happiness this time, that her child was safe. She also knew that he was no ordinary child and would always be able to beat all odds.

If you give something your best shot and try sincerely, you will surely be successful.

18

So many complaints against Krishna

Has anyone ever come to your mother and complained about you? Isn't it scary?

Not just you and me, but gods have also had their share of punishments, it seems. Krishna was such a naughty child that someone or the other always came and complained to Yashoda about him. She was a simple woman who did not believe the complaints in the beginning, but later, she started wondering… what if they were true?

One such day, she decided to find out the truth. Let's read what happened after that. Was little Krishna really punished?

It was a bright and sunny day and the kids were out playing. As Yashoda mentally made a note of what had to be made for lunch, she heard a knock at her door. There were about five women, all from the neighbourhood, waiting to come in.

She invited them in and offered them some fresh, cool water. When they had settled, Yashoda asked them why they all looked so worried. One of the women started telling Yashoda how Krishna had been stealing butter from her house, drinking all the milk, and buttermilk too. They did not have a problem offering it to him if he asked for it, but they did not like the fact that he stole it.

Yashoda argued that her house had a cowshed with many cows. There was so much butter and milk that Krishna need not steal. But given the continuous complaints from entire Gokul, she decided to go with them and check. The women were more than happy, because they were sure that they could catch Krishna red-handed. And the same happened too. In one of the houses in the village, the women and Yashoda saw Krishna climbing up an old stool to reach the butter in a pot hanging from the hook. His toli of friends was with him too. Yashoda was angry and very shocked. She had never expected Krishna to do such a thing.

Yashoda did not say anything to anyone, but held Krishna by the arm and took him home with her. She asked him several times why he stole when he could have enough at home. But he just continued to smile, without an answer.

She decided to not ignore it this time, and punish him. But what punishment could she give? Hmm, she decided to tie him up to an *okhli* (a mortar, a cup shaped vessel to crush grains/ spices). She also thought she would keep him in the sun and make him sweat a bit. Maybe that would make Krishna realize that stealing was a bad thing.

She took a rope, made Krishna stand next to the okhli and tried to tie him. The rope was slightly small. She took a bigger piece of rope and tried to wrap it around his waist to tie him up. But the rope was again an inch short. She tied both the ropes together, sure that this would be long enough. But she was shocked that this rope was also an inch short. How could this be?

She was tired of sitting in the sun and was on the verge of tears. She looked at Krishna; he was smiling, like always. When Krishna saw tears in his mother's eyes, he felt sorry that he had hurt her so much. He said sorry to her and asked her to tie him now. Krishna also said he realized that stealing was bad, but he had been taking butter only because those women and people had offered it to him first.

Krishna smiled and asked her to tie him. She knew that it was one of his tricks that she could not tie him. But now

when she tried, she could tie him. As if the rope needed Krishna's permission to be long enough.

Yashoda gave up on tying him and hugged him instead, and Krishna promised he would not steal anymore.

It takes years to earn our parents' and friends' trust. We must be very careful of what we do, and how.

Let's help little Krishna to find the lotus

Draupadi

She was born out of a fire in a yajna

She is also seen as an incarnation of devi, especially Parvati

She was brought up by king Drupad and queen Prishataa

She is worshipped as Draupadi Amman in southern India

Her siblings were Drishtadyumna, Shikhandi and Satyajit

She was married to the Pandava brothers

19

Born out of fire

King Drupad of Panchal kingdom was a mighty warrior, but was defeated in battle by the Pandavas. He was furious after the defeat, and also impressed with Arjun's might. This dual feeling led to the birth of Draupadi. She is known to be the most beautiful woman in the epic *Mahabharata* who is a warrior princess, excelling in the art of wisdom, warfare and weaponry. Unlike other children, she was born out of fire, and that's why she also had a fiery, burning temperament. Let us read the story of her birth.

Drupad and Drona were best friends – the former a kshatriya prince, the latter a brahmin. Drupad promised Drona that when they grew up, he would give Drona half his kingdom. Unfortunately by the time they grew up, Drupad had forgotten all about the promise. It annoyed Drona a lot that despite reminding, Drupad did not want to fulfil his promise.

To take revenge, Drona went to the Kuru kingdom and established himself there as the teacher for the Kuru princes and Pandavas. He used to teach them the use of weapons. When the princes had become experts in the use of weapons, Drona sought their help to defeat Drupad and win over his kingdom as *guru dakshina* (the fee for training them).

As a result, the Pandavas defeated Drupad and won over his kingdom. Though Drona forgave him and returned half the kingdom, keeping the other half, Drupad could not forget the insult. He realized he couldn't win because he had no young children to fight for him. So he decided to performe a putrakameshti yajna (a ritual praying for children).

He performed sincere prayers to seek two children from the gods – a son who could defeat Drona in battle, and a daughter who could marry a great warrior like Arjun and rule the world.

On the day of the yajna, there were many good omens that indicated to Drupad that his wish would be fulfilled. As the sages and brahmins started chanting mantras, the agni (fire in the havan kund) kept growing mightier and higher. It seemed as if the god of fire, Agni dev, was himself a part of the ritual.

Soon, everyone saw a young boy emerging out of the fire. Drupad was happy to have received a son as radiant as him, and named him Drishtadyumna.

Then everyone saw the fire reaching higher than ever, shining so bright that you couldn't look into it. A beautiful, dark-skinned young girl emerged from the fire. She wasn't a child, but a full-grown woman, beautiful and powerful. Along with her birth, there was an *akashvani* (a heavenly announcement) telling everyone present that this girl would change the future of the country, which was then called Bharatvarsh.

She came to be known by many names: Krishnaa, because of her dark complexion; Yajnaseni, as she was born out of the yajna fire, Panchali, because she was the princess of Panchal, and the most well-known of all – Draupadi, the daughter of Drupad.

As we all know, she later went on to marry Arjun and the other Pandavas, and also brought about a great change in the future of the country, after the battle of Kurukshetra.

Draupadi was born out of the fire, but we – you and I – don't need fire to make us fiery and passionate. All we need is an inner fire, a goal and the will to work towards it, to keep us going.

20

Draupadi plays the dice game

The epic *Mahabharata* is a complicated story of many kingdoms, kings, and various battles, with the Pandavas at the core. I am sure you know that a dice game became the turning point for the Kauravas and Pandavas and changed the dynamics of Bharatvarsh as a nation. The rulers became losers and they had to fight for their own share of kingdom. But do you know, that there are several versions of the story where things are different. Let us read the following folk tale from Karnataka which changes the ending of this life-changing event.

The Pandavas were righteous rulers – they did not take undue advantage of anyone, and they also never cheated anyone. But the same could not be said for the others around them. As is common in big kingdoms and politics, there were a few people, looking for an opportunity to take advantage.

Duryodhan (one of the hundred Kuru princes) had always been very jealous of his cousin brothers, the five Pandavas. He wanted to be the king after his father, and decided to do something to get the five brothers out of his way.

So he made a plan, along with his uncle Shakuni. They decided to invite Yudhishthir for a game of dice. They knew he had a soft corner for the game and wouldn't say no. That's what they wanted to take advantage of.

The day was decided. The stage was set. The court was full. The game was on!

When they started playing, Yudhishthir kept winning. That also encouraged him to bet more and play more. Little did he know that it was a part of Shakuni's plan. Once the game was at its peak, Duryodhan and Shakuni started playing their real game.

They teased Yudhishthir to bet more, and laughed at him for being so scared of playing. Excited by their words, he bet his entire kingdom. And lost. It was a shock, his losing the bet after winning for so long. To make him continue and not give up, Shakuni prompted him to bet something else, and win everything back in one go.

In the grip of passion and anxious to win everything back, Yudhishthir bet himself and his brothers in the game too. As was planned by Duryodhan, Yudhishthir lost again. Now the Pandavas had lost all their kingdom, and were Duryodhan's and Shakuni's property – literally, their slaves.

What had started as a fun game had suddenly changed into a battle. And the Pandavas had lost without fighting. While all this was happening in the court, one of the servants ran to Draupadi and informed her of the events. She was sure Yudhishthir had been trapped by the Kauravas and decided to take control.

At that time, it wasn't common for royal women to make themselves seen in front of the public. But forgetting all that, Draupadi marched right into a hall full of people. One look at the Pandavas and she knew that all was lost. Yudhishthir was about to bet Draupadi too, but she stopped him in time.

We must know here that according to Ved Vyasa's *Mahabharata*, Yudhishthir lost Draupadi in the bet too, after which she was insulted in front of the whole court. But in a Kannada folk version of the same event, Draupadi turns the tables. She proves herself to be every bit the confident warrior princess that she was born to be.

She stopped Yudhishthir from betting her, and addressed Duryodhan and Shakuni. She blamed them for having

cheated their brother into playing, knowing fully well that this was one game he passionately liked but had no mastery over.

She challenged the duo to play with her, sure that she would beat them to dust. Duryodhan burnt with anger to be addressed like this in his own court. In a fit of rage, he accepted the challenge and asked Shakuni to play further.

The only bet was – if Draupadi won, everything that Yudhishthir had lost till now would get back to him; and if she lost, the Pandavas and Draupadi would surrender themselves and their kingdom in the service of the Kauravas. A rather tempting offer!

Everyone in the hall held their breath as the dice rolled. Duryodhan was quite distracted looking at Draupadi. She was the most beautiful woman and he was not able to concentrate on the game as she sat right opposite. Draupadi realized this and at a crucial point in the game, when she saw Duryodhan's attention was more on her and less on the game, she rolled the dice.

The entire hall went silent. Draupadi had beaten Duryodhan and won everything back for the Pandavas. After this, she graciously left the court with the Pandavas, leaving Duryodhan and Shakuni to mourn the loss of opportunity.

We don't always win battles by our physical powers; sometimes the mind is enough to play the winning stroke.

21

The last grain of rice

We all know that in Vyasa's *Mahabharata*, the Pandavas and Draupadi had to spend twelve years in vanvas (exile). That is, they had to roam around and live in the forests, instead of their royal palace.

As a child, I often wondered how the Pandavas always found their food. Wouldn't it be tough to find something to eat? Or kill animals for food all the time? That's when my father told me about the 'Akshay patra'. It was a small bowl that could produce unlimited food. Till Draupadi ate and concluded the meal, it would keep giving as much food as they wanted. Isn't that amazing?

Let's see why Draupadi could not offer any food to several rishis when they came to her hut.

After losing their kingdom and freedom to the Kauravas, the Pandavas were forced into an exile (vanwas) for twelve years. As a pre-condition, they could not stay at any one place for too long, and had to keep moving from one forest to another.

The food requirements were taken care of by the Akshay patra – the vessel that never ran out of food. It had been given to Yudhishthir by Sun god and proved to be such a blessing. The only catch was – it stopped giving out food for the day after Draupadi concluded her meal.

Now, sage Durvasa was a very renowned rishi, who was also known for his short temper. One day, he visited Duryodhan in Hastinapur. Duryodhan respectfully took care of him and the other rishis, and offered them a hearty meal. Sage Durvasa was very happy and blessed him.

Just then, Duryodhan told the rishi that the Pandavas were in a nearby forest too, and he could visit them. Duryodhan knew well that by the time the sages reached the Pandavas, they would be hungry again. And Draupadi would have eaten, so the Akshya patra would not be of any help. This was a perfect plan!

Sage Durvasa really wanted to see the Pandavas, so he and the other rishis started off towards their hut. As

Duryodhan had guessed, they all reached the hut tired and hungry. The Pandavas were happy to receive them, and respectfully seated them, preparing to offer food.

Draupadi knew that the Akshay patra would not give her any food, now that she had eaten. She was really sad at the thought that the sages would have to be hungry till the Pandavas could find more food. She also did not want the rishis to be angry with her and the Pandavas.

So she prayed to lord Krishna to help her. She knew only he could show her a way out in this situation. When she opened her eyes, to her surprise, Krishna stood right in front of her. She told him the problem, but he kept smiling. She was a little surprised as to why Krishna was smiling and not helping her.

Then Krishna asked her to check if the Akshay patra was actually empty. She said it was. He asked Draupadi to check again, properly. She handed him the bowl and repeated that there was nothing in it. Krishna put his hand inside the vessel and dug out a single grain of rice stuck to the side. He ate the single grain and felt gratified.

Magically, all the rishis suddenly felt well rested and full. They told the Pandavas they were not hungry and had just come to bless them. They left soon after. And so did Krishna, having taught Draupadi an essential lesson – if the bhakta offers even a single grain of rice to god, with sincerity and love, the god feels fulfilled.

Like that, in life, if we put some effort – but sincere effort – we have higher chances of success than spending years over doing something half-heartedly. Think about it!

Heroes and heroines in Indian mythology

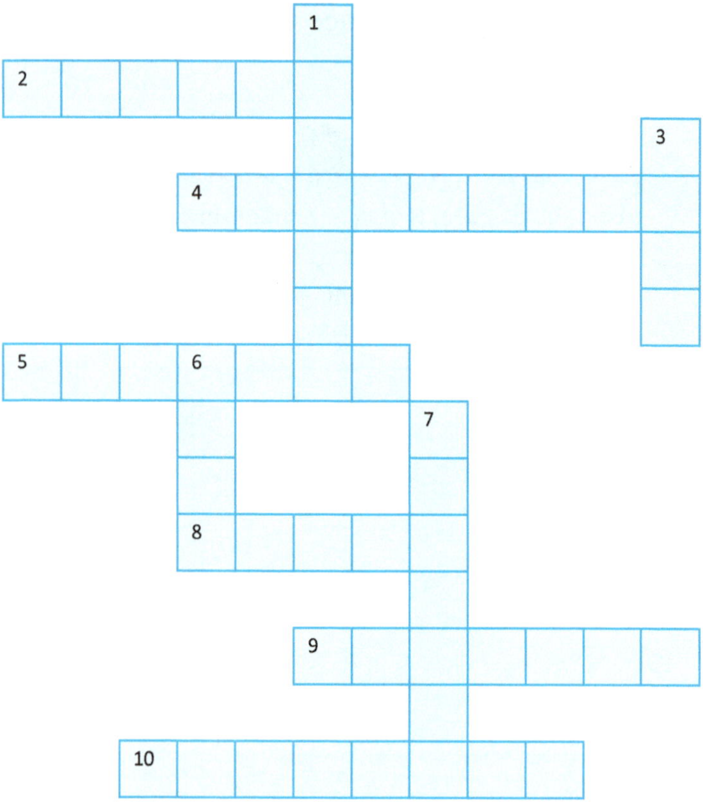

Across

2. His name means a loud roar, and he was a well-known bhakta of Shiva
4. Mother of the crown prince of Ayodhya
5. The blue god who is adored by everyone
8. An archer par excellence, he could hit a fish's eye from a distance
9. Biological father of a god, who was brought up by Nanda and Yashoda
10. The queen who was born out of fire

Down

1. He jumped across an entire ocean
3. He lived in the forest for years and was an ideal ruler
6. A warrior princess who was kidnapped by the Rakshas king
7. He is always the first to be worshipped; he loves laddus

Pandavas

Pandavas were five brothers – Yudhishthir, Arjun, Bhima, Nakul and Sahadev

The Pandavas established the Indraprastha city, now known as Delhi

They were the sons of king Pandu and queens Kunti and Madri

They lived in exile in a forest for twelve years

They fought the Mahabharata war in Kurukshetra against Kauravas

22

Arjun and the crocodiles

The epics – *Ramayana* and *Mahabharata* – are full of unheard stories of magical creatures, gods and goddesses, demons and apsaras and strange curses. As a story, the *Mahabharata* is much more complicated, because it has many stories within stories. It's like a never-ending magic box of tales.

The following story has Arjun and fairies and crocodiles and sages. Let us see how the master storyteller Vyasa has woven these together.

As you have read earlier in the chapter on Draupadi, the Pandavas in exile kept moving from one forest to another. Towards the end of their exile years, they all knew very well that they would need some divine weapons to fight with the mighty Kuru army, which included not just their own brothers, but teachers too.

So Arjun went to the Himalayas in order to perform tapasya, to win over some weapons from the gods. On his way, he met many rishis and visited many ashrams. Everyone was keen on meeting Arjun, because he was a celebrated warrior of the country. Some sages also sought his help for matters pertaining to their safety, and Arjun was happy to help.

Once, he reached an ashram on the foothills of the mountains. The sages were very happy to receive him. They offered him a place to rest, clean clothes and fresh food. It helped him a great deal, but after walking through forests for days, he really wanted to have a bath. On asking about some river or pond close to the ashram, all the sages became hesitant.

One of the rishis told Arjun that there were five fresh water ponds around the ashram. But they could not go to any of them, because all five had a crocodile each living in it. And the crocodiles were fierce and violent, that the rishis have to avoid going there to save their lives. They requested Arjun to help them.

Arjun was angry to know that a bunch of crocodiles had become so fearless that they attacked such peace-loving people. He set out to kill them and help the rishis. As it is, Arjun had a boon from Ulupi – the snake-king's daughter – that no creature living in water would ever be able to defeat Arjun.

When he reached the pool, he was awed by the beauty of the place. It was so peaceful and the water of the pond so clear and cool. He slowly stepped into the water, his senses alert to any movement around him. Within a few seconds, he sensed some movement to his left, and turned abruptly to see a huge crocodile coming towards him.

With its open mouth and sharp teeth, the crocodile looked scary. But Arjun was confident. So he used all his power and held the crocodile's mouth open with his hands. Soon, he had overpowered the crocodile and captured it.

Arjun slowly dragged the crocodile to the edge of the pond, but oh! The crocodile changed into a beautiful woman. Arjun was so confused. One moment back, he was fighting with a crocodile; and now it had become a girl!

The beautiful woman told Arjun that her name was Varga and she was an apsara from Kuber's court. She, and four of her friends, had been cursed by a sage for disturbing his tapasya. They had all become crocodiles in the ponds

around the area. The sage had told them that the warrior who was able to defeat the crocodiles would be able to set the apsaras free from the curse.

Varga then requested Arjun to free the other four apsaras too, which he did. They all thanked him and left the pond safe for the rishis once again.

I personally feel it is great to be able to help someone. But we must know our own strengths and weaknesses before we set out to change the world. Conquer your inner self before winning over the world.

23

Yaksha questions the Pandavas

What's the worst punishment you can think of if you fail to answer your teacher's questions? And what happens when you cannot answer your parents satisfactorily? Oh, and what if it is a competition and you really want to answer and win? Hmm, think about it!

But would you be this serious if a bird started asking you some questions?

In the story that follows, a crane wants to quiz the Pandava brothers on some philosophical questions, but nobody wants to answer, it seems. The result can be disastrous. Let's see what happens in this strange situation.

It was the end of the twelve years of exile and the Pandavas were preparing for the incognito stay of one year – which meant they had to hide their real identity for one year in a new place. While traveling in search of a suitable place, the Pandavas came across a brahmin, who asked for their help. He told them that a deer had run away with his fire-creating wooden blocks. Without them, he'd be unable to cook his food and survive in the forest.

The Pandavas decided to help him and went in search of the deer. With the passage of time, they got really tired and sat down to rest. Yudhishthir was very thirsty and asked Sahadev to search for some water around them. Sahadev was the youngest and set out to look for water. He came across a pond of cool water, and bent down to drink some when a crane standing there warned him – 'If you drink this water without answering my questions, the water will become poisonous.'

Sahadev was thirsty and did not pay heed to the words. Shortly after sipping the water, he fell down unconscious. When he did not return for long, Nakul set out to look for him. Sadly, he met the same fate at the edge of the pond. Slowly, Arjun and Bhima also came looking for the other brothers, and fell prey to their pride. None of them paid attention to the words of the crane.

In the end, having waited for his brothers for very long, Yudhishthir reached the pond. On seeing all his brothers lying unconscious, he was shocked. That's when he heard the crane say the same words - 'If you drink this water without answering my questions, the water will become poisonous. Your brothers did not listen to me and met this fate. If you wish to see them again, you have to answer me.'

Yudhishthir realized it was not just a bird, but a *yaksha*, a nature spirit. He decided to answer all his questions. So the yaksha smiled, revealed his true form and started asking.

Yaksha: How can one become educated? And how can one become wise?

Yudhishtir thought a bit and said: We learn through the scriptures, but intelligence comes through serving our elders and learning from their experience.

Yaksha: What is heavier than the earth, higher than the heavens above, and faster than the wind?

Yudhishthir: A mother carries more weight than the earth; the father is higher than the heavens; and the mind is faster than the wind.

Yaksha: Who is an ill man's friend?

Yudhishthir: A doctor or a medicine man.

Yaksha: And the friend of a dying man?

Yudhishthir: Charity and good deeds.

Yaksha: Giving up on what can make one lovable?

Yudhishthir: Pride.

Yaksha: And what's one enemy that is unbeatable?
Yudhishthir: Anger.

The yaksha asked Yudhishthir eighteen complicated, philosophical questions, and he answered them satisfactorily. The yaksha offered to revive one of his brothers in return, but not all. Yudhishthir chose Nakul, because he was his stepbrother. He wanted to ensure that his stepmother did not have to see the end of both her children.

The yaksha was so happy at his selfless reply that he gave life back to all the four brothers and blessed them for victory in all their tasks.

Sometimes, our pride is our biggest enemy. We can ignore people's words in our pride and pay a heavy price. There is no better tool than communication to keep our relationships and the world going great!

References:

The stories presented in the book have been taken from various versions of the epics, including but not limited to: *Valmiki's Ramayana, Ramcharitamanas, Adbhuta Ramayana, Krittibasi Ramayan, Kamba Ramayan, Vyasa's Mahabharata* and its derivatives, Yakshagana performances, Patachitra scrolls, folk, performative and oral traditions from across India, Pandav Lila tradition from Uttarakhand, etc.

Picture and Illustrations credits:

Ishan Trivedi: 4, 10, 14, 22, 27, 32, 34, 41, 46, 50, 53, 58, 62, 72, 77, 82, 90, 94, 100, 103, 107, 113, 117, 126, 131.

Designed by Mithaas Services: 2, 18, 38, 54, 68, 86, 104, 122.

Shutterstock: 1, 17, 67, 68, 85, 86, 102.

Designed by Freepik: v, vi.

Public domain: 37 (Wikimedia commons), 121 (Wikimedia commons).

While due care has been taken to put together credits for pictures and illustrations used in the book at press time, any inadvertent miss shall be rectified in subsequent prints after it is brought to our notice.

For solutions to puzzles in the book, scan the QR code

About the author

Stuti's tryst with stories and storytelling started as soon as she learnt to talk. Now she enjoys writing stories for children and passing on the magic of tales to bright, young minds.

This is her third book after she introduced *101 Best Indian Fables for Children* and compiled *Popular Indian Fairy Tales* from the heart of Indian story traditions.

She has an M.Phil degree in literature from the University of Delhi, and more than a dozen years of experience with stories and content-related work.

She loves to read, talk and make learning fun. She tests all her stories on her three-year-old before sharing them with the world.

She can be reached at storytellerstuti@gmail.com

: @stuti_vg : /StorytellerStuti